Phonics
Activity Book

for ages 5-6

This CGP book is full of fun activities
to build up children's skills and confidence.

It's ideal for extra practice to reinforce their
learning in primary school. Enjoy!

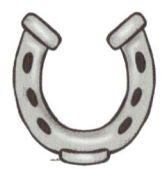 # Hints for Helpers

Here are a few useful things to know when using this book:

- This book covers **Phase Five** of most **systematic synthetic phonics programmes**. It helps children to practise common sounds from the English language and recognise the letters that can be used to write these sounds.

- Your child's teacher will introduce the main ways of spelling each sound over a term or more. A key part of Phonics learning is **practice**, so you might want to use this book in short bursts to **reinforce** what they're learning at school.

- The first 10 pages of this book help children to learn **alternative pronunciations** of letters (e.g. **i** sounds different in 'f**i**nd' and 'p**i**n'). The rest of the book encourages them to recognise and practise different ways of **spelling sounds** (e.g. the "igh" sound is spelt differently in 'h**igh**' and 'fr**y**').

- The book is designed to be worked through in **order**. However, the 'Space adventures' activity in the centre uses sounds from **throughout the book**. You may want to complete this activity **last**.

- As you work through the book, it may be useful to ask your child to **identify** the **sounds** in the words they read, and/or the letters that are making each **sound**.

- If your child comes across an unfamiliar word, you can help by **reading** it to them and encouraging them to **copy** the **sounds** you make.

Published by CGP

Editors: Andy Cashmore, Robbie Driscoll, Georgina Paxman, Kirsty Sweetman

With thanks to Emma Crighton, Sharon Gulliver and Lucy Towle for the proofreading.

With thanks to Emily Smith for the copyright research.

ISBN: 978 1 78908 891 5

Printed by Elanders Ltd, Newcastle upon Tyne.
Cover and graphics used throughout the book © Educlips
Cover design concept by emc design ltd.

Text, design, layout and original illustrations
© Coordination Group Publications Ltd. (CGP) 2022
All rights reserved.

Photocopying this book is not permitted, even if you have a CLA licence.
Extra copies are available from CGP with next day delivery • 0800 1712 712 • www.cgpbooks.co.uk

Contents

i, o and e	2
u and a	4
c, g and ch	6
ea, ow and ie	8
y, er and ou	10
"f", "w" and "s" sounds	12
"e", "i" and "o" sounds	14
"or", "ar" and "ur" sounds	16
Space adventures	18
"j" and "ch" sounds	20
"ear" and "air" sounds	22
"ow" and "oa" sounds	24
"oi" and "ai" sounds	26
Short "u" and short "oo" sounds	28
Long "oo" and "yoo" sounds	30
"ee" and "igh" sounds	32
"sh", "zh" and "z" sounds	34
Answers	36

i, o and e

How It Works

The letters **i**, **o** and **e** make different sounds in different words. Read each pair of words out loud.

w**i**ng   f**i**nd   fr**o**g   **o**pen

sp**e**ll   **e**vil

Now Try These

1. Read the words below out loud. The letter **i** makes a different sound in each word. Draw lines to match each word to the correct picture.

wizard

child

2. Practise saying the words below. The letter **o** makes a different sound in each word. Draw lines to match each word to the correct picture.

monster

ghost

3. Colour the pictures that contain the same sound as the **e** in **spell**.

elf   dream   well

4. Circle the word that contains the same sound as the **e** in **evil**.

web   me   step

An Extra Challenge

Willow the witch is using some strange things to make a potion. Can you read the words out loud? What sounds do they have?

Did you work your magic on those sounds? Tick a box.

u and a

How It Works

The letter **u** makes a different sound in different words. Say these words.

tr**u**mpet

m**u**sic

The letter **a** can also make different sounds. Read these words out loud.

pi**a**no

r**a**dio

w**a**tch

Now Try These

1. Say these words. Circle the word that has the same sound as the **a** in **radio**.

harp

tap

paper

2. Say these words. Colour the word that has the same sound as the **u** in **music**.

hum

uniform

sound

jump

3. Read the word below out loud. Does the letter **u** have the same sound as the **u** in **trumpet** or the **u** in **music**? Draw a line to match it to the correct picture.

drum

4. Read the sentences below out loud. Circle the word that has the same sound as the **a** in **watch**.

He likes to rap.

She wants to sing.

I play a tune.

An Extra Challenge

Cleo is singing a song and needs help saying the words properly. Can you work out if each underlined letter below sounds like the **a** in **piano**, **radio** or **watch**?

I feel h<u>a</u>ppy when I sing.

Singing is an am<u>a</u>zing thing.

Smile and cl<u>a</u>p and t<u>a</u>p along.

That's wh<u>a</u>t makes a joyful song.

Did you stay in tune with those tricky questions? Tick a box.

c, g and ch

How It Works

The letters **c** and **g** can make different sounds. Say each pair of words below.

cleaner   poli**c**e   **g**olf   ma**g**ic

The letters **ch** make different sounds in different words too. Say these words.

tea**ch**er   me**ch**anic   **ch**ef

Now Try These

1. Read the words below out loud, making sure you say the letter **g** correctly each time. Then, match each word to the person who works there.

   garden   garage   gym

2. Colour in the words that contain the same sound as the **c** in **cleaner**.

cereal   rice

carrots   cabbage

3. Say the sentences below. Find the **ch** word in each one, then write down whether the **ch** has the same sound as in **teacher**, **mechanic** or **chef**.

Jo had a tooth ache. ....

Bart helps children. ....

Sita uses machines. ....

An Extra Challenge

Mr Miles is teaching a lesson.

Which words on his whiteboard contain the same sound as the **g** in **golf**?

Which one contains the same sound as the **g** in **magic**?

gold   grey
blue
green
pink   orange

Have you been hard at work with these pages? Tick a box.

ea, ow and ie

How It Works

The letters **ea** can make different sounds. Try saying these words.

leaf

w**ea**ther

The letters **ow** can make different sounds too. Now say these words.

gr**ow**

fl**ow**er

The letters **ie** can also make different sounds. Practise reading these words out loud.

p**ie**

f**ie**ld

Now Try These

1. Circle the word that contains the same sound as the **ea** in **weather**.

heap

bean

dead

2. Can you say these words? Does each word contain the same sound as the **ie** in **pie** or the **ie** in **field**?

ch**ie**f   repl**ie**d   bel**ie**ve

3. Say the sentences below. Find the **ow** word in each one, then write down whether the **ow** has the same sound as in **grow** or **flower**.

Dex mows the grass. ....

The tree fell down. ....

They saw a cow. ....

4. Draw lines to match the words that contain the same sound. The first one has been done for you.

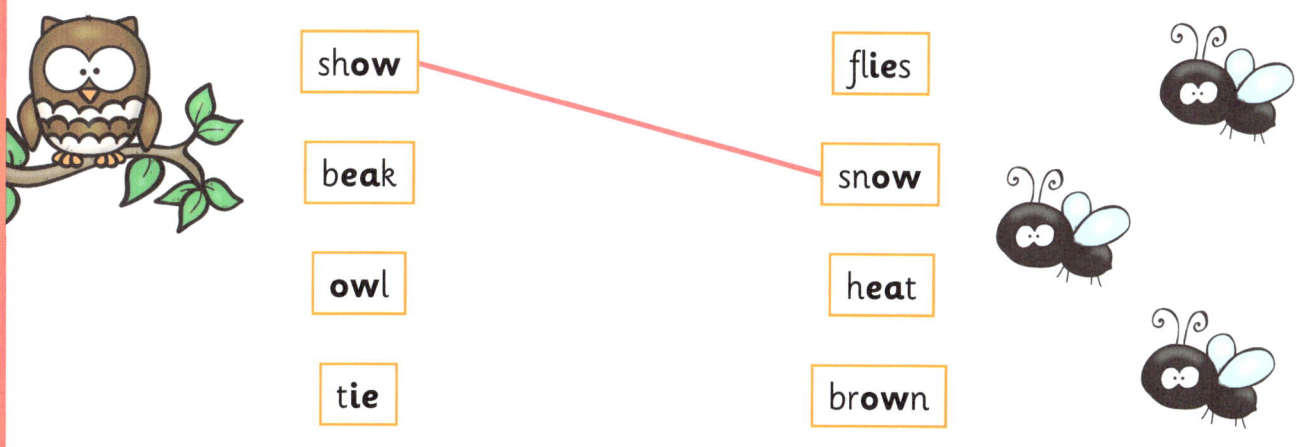

show — snow

beak

owl

tie

flies

heat

brown

An Extra Challenge

Mira has four things on her window sill that contain the letters **ea**. Name each thing, then say whether each one has the same sound as the **ea** in **leaf** or the **ea** in **weather**.

Are these sounds growing on you? Give a box a tick.

y, er and ou

How It Works

The letter **y** makes different sounds in different words. Say these words.

yard   hea**vy**   sk**y**

The letters **er** can make different sounds too. Next, say these words.

The letters **ou** can also make different sounds. Here are some of them:

wat**er**   h**er**b   gr**ou**nd   s**ou**p

Now Try These

1. Circle the word that contains the same sound as the **y** in **sky**.

 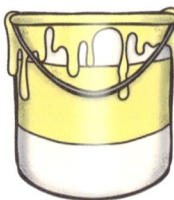 

| messy | yellow | dry |

2. Colour the boxes with words that have the same sound as the **ou** in **ground**.

| house | group | you | count |

3. Put a tick under the words that have the same sound as the **er** in **herb**.

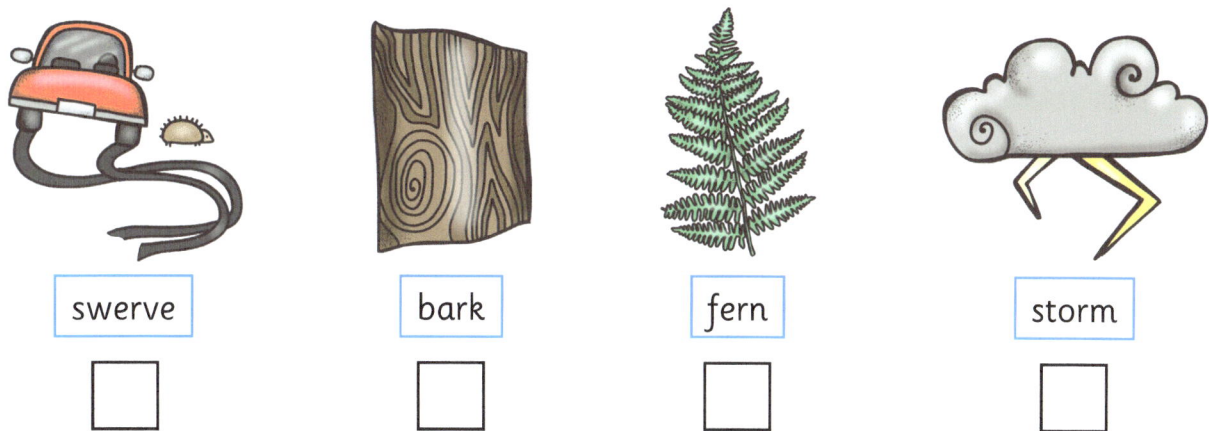

| swerve | bark | fern | storm |

☐ ☐ ☐ ☐

4. Fill in the gaps in the sentences below with
   y, **er** or **ou**, then read the sentences out loud.

My drill is l........d.

 That is my spann......... .

The nails are rust......... .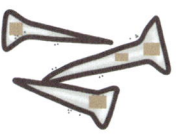

An Extra Challenge

The picture shows the equipment that Lena is using to design a new house. How many things can you spot that have the same sound as the **er** in **water**?

You've really hit the nail on the head there! Give a box a tick.

 ☐  ☐  ☐

"f", "w" and "s" sounds

How It Works

Say these words. They use different spellings to make the "f" sound.

Now try saying these words. They both have the "w" sound.

four   al**ph**abet   **w**ork   **wh**isper

Now say these words. They all use different spellings to make the "s" sound.

school   **c**ity   hou**se**

These are just some of the ways of writing the "s" sound.

Now Try These

1. Draw a line from each object to the sound it contains, then circle the letters in the word that make this sound.

  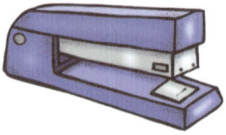 

graph   pencil   stapler   folder

 "f"   "s"

2. Here is what Jess had for her packed lunch at school. Practise saying these words, then underline the letter that makes the "s" sound in each one.

strawberry

sandwich

juice

3. Find the words that contain the "w" sound in the sentence below and write them on the dotted lines. Then, underline the letters that make the sound.

When the whistle sounded, Will's team won.

....

....

An Extra Challenge

Kai is getting ready for a spelling test. To help him practise, he is making a list of words with **ph** in. How many more words can you think of to add to his list?

dolphin

sphere

Was that as easy as ABC? Tick a box to show what you know.

"e", "i" and "o" sounds

How It Works

Say the two words below.
Both words have the "e" sound.

Now say these words.
Both words have the "i" sound.

j**e**t   sw**ea**t   l**i**ck   s**y**rup

Here's one more pair of words for you to say.   Both words have the "o" sound.

l**o**lly   w**a**sp

Now Try These

1. What sound can you hear in the word **wash**? Circle the right answer.

   the "e" sound   the "o" sound   the "i" sound

2. Which of these words contains the same sound as the **a** in **wash**?
   Circle the right answer.

  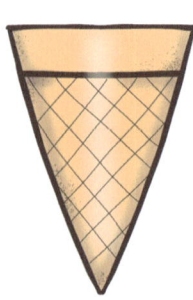

melt   drop   cone

3. Colour the pictures that contain the "e" sound.

| tub | head | pet | sun |

4. Underline the words in the sentence below that contain the "i" sound. Then, write them on the dotted lines.

> Tim solved the mystery of the missing chips.

....

....

An Extra Challenge

Raj has made a poster to advertise his ice cream stall.
How many words can you spot in the poster that contain the "e" sound?

Fresh Ice Cream
Are you ready for the best ice cream in town? Ten heavenly flavours to take your breath away!

Are you the cream of the crop?
Tick a box to show how you did.

"or", "ar" and "ur" sounds

How It Works

Have a go at saying the words below.
They all use different spellings to make the "or" sound.

These are just some of the ways of writing each sound.

p**aw**   **au**tumn   p**our**

Now say these words out loud.
They all have the "ar" sound.

Practise saying these words.
Each word has the "ur" sound.

ban**a**na   h**a**lf   b**ir**d   **ear**th

Now Try These

1. Say the words below. Circle the sound you can hear in all three words.

walk   snore   thorn

 "ar"

 "or"

2. Practise saying these sentences. Circle the word in each sentence that contains the "ar" sound.

Leo went camping with his father .

It gets dark at night .

3. Circle the words that contain the "ur" sound.

| hurt | stump | girl | jar |

4. Read the sentences below out loud. What sound can you hear in each orange word? Draw a line to match each sentence to the right sound.

The lake was **calm**.

It is **four** o'clock.

Meg **heard** a noise.

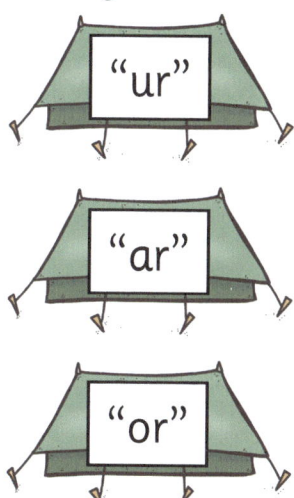

"ur"

"ar"

"or"

An Extra Challenge

Eve is trying to get to the campsite using these directions.

Read the directions out loud.

How many words can you spot that contain an "ar" sound?

How many words can you spot that contain an "ur" sound?

Turn left out of the car park next to a large fir tree. Walk along the path to the waterfall. The campsite is in the farm on your right.

Are you a happy camper?
Tick a box to show how you did.

Space adventures

Greetings! Can you help Zig the alien send each rocket to the right planets? Say each word out loud and think about the sounds it contains.

Colour the planets with the "yoo" sound red, the planets with the "igh" sound blue, the planets with the "ee" sound yellow, and the planets with the "or" sound green. Then, underline the letters in each word that make the sound.

You'll need the sounds from pages 16, 30 and 32 to do these activities.

"yoo" "igh" "ee" "or"

belief   rescue   shine   orbit

human   galaxy   launch   mind

fumes   dream   skies   claw

future   flight   deep   astronaut

Look at the picture of Zig the alien, then read the sentences out loud. Can you work out if they are true or false? Tick the true sentences.

Zig meets a space explorer.

The flag is red and blue.

Zig is wearing a space suit.

There is a moon in the sky. ☐

Bonus: Read the sentences above again. Can you spot three words that contain the long "oo" sound? Write them on the dotted lines below.

....

"j" and "ch" sounds

How It Works

Say the words with the "j" sound below. Each word has a different spelling.

jeep   bri**dge**   **g**em

Try saying these words too. Each word has the "ch" sound.

chair   ha**tch**   pi**c**ture

Now Try These

1. Here are some animals Ben saw on his safari trip. Colour the animal that starts with the "j" sound.

monkey   vulture   giraffe   cheetah

2. The words below are missing some sounds. Fill in the gaps with either **dge** or **tch** to complete the words.

sna............   ske............   fri............

3. Fill the gap in each sentence with the word that contains the "j" sound.

Larry the lion is in a .... church cage

Larry hid behind a .... hedge chair

Larry .... on a log. jumped stretched

4. Draw a line to match each word to the sound it contains.

nature

scratch

jungle

danger

creature

"j"

"ch"

An Extra Challenge

Here is the menu at 'Tina's Treehouse Cafe'.
How many words can you spot that contain the "j" or "ch" sounds?
Can you think of any more foods with these sounds?

Jam on toast
Tina's signature salad
Chicken and chips
Pumpkin patch pie
Spicy potato wedges

Was this page an adventure?
Give a box a tick.

"ear" and "air" sounds

How It Works

Have a go at saying the words below. They all contain the "ear" sound.

sph**ere**   b**ear**d   ch**eer**s

Now say these words. Each one has a different spelling of the "air" sound.

p**air**   b**ear**   h**are**   th**ere**

Now Try These

1. Draw lines to match each word below to the sound it contains.

earmuffs   bare   reindeer   wear

"ear"   "air"

2. Find the word that contains an "ear" sound, and colour in its glove.

 dare    year    where    pear

3. Circle the two words that are missing the "air" sound.

ch<u>air</u>

sc<u>a</u>f

f<u>ire</u>

sc<u>are</u>d

An Extra Challenge

Patrick is having a snowball fight with his friends. Can you find the odd word out in each group of snowballs? Think about the sounds they contain.

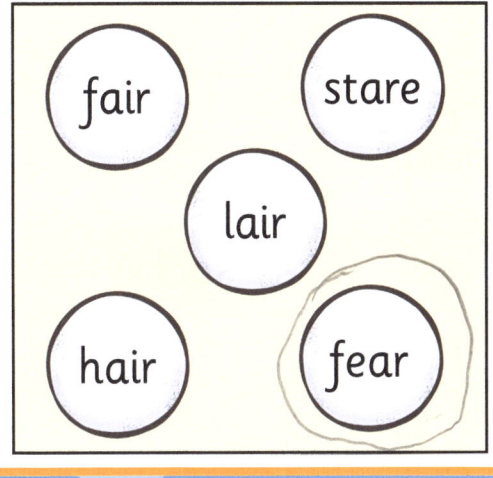

fair   stare   lair   hair   fear

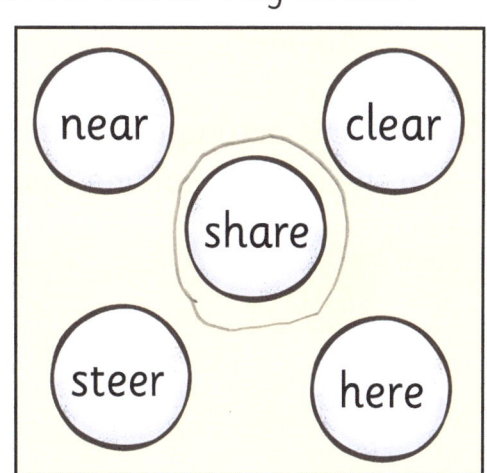

near   clear   share   steer   here

Did you skate through those pages? Tick a box.

"ow" and "oa" sounds

How It Works

Say these words. Each word uses a different spelling to make the "ow" sound.

fr**ow**n

bl**ou**se

Now say these words. They all contain the "oa" sound.

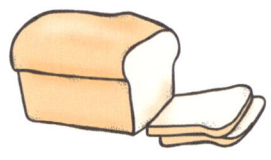
l**oa**f

pill**ow**

w**o**k**e**

In 'woke', the **o** and the **e** work together to make the "oa" sound, even though they are split apart.

Now Try These

1. Colour the words below that contain the "oa" sound.

cereal   toast   below

   milk   home

2. Archie is getting dressed. Draw a line from Archie to the item of clothing that contains the "ow" sound.

shirt   socks

jumper   trousers

3. Can you spot the "ow" sound in each word below?
   Circle the letters used to make the sound.

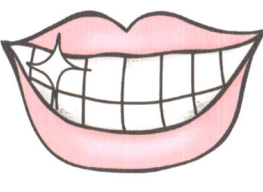

towel   shower   mouth

4. Read the sentences below out loud.
   Put a tick next to the sentences that contain a word with the "oa" sound in.

He put his coat on.

She waved from the window.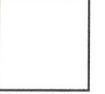

They were running late.

An Extra Challenge

Maisie has taken some photos of things she saw on her walk to school. Can you work out if the thing in each photo has the "ow" sound or the "oa" sound?

cloud   scarecrow   mouse   rainbow   fountain

What a day! Have you perfected those sounds?

"oi" and "ai" sounds

How It Works

Have a go at saying the words below. They both contain the "oi" sound.

co**i**n   **b**oy

Now say these words. Each one has a different spelling of the "ai" sound.

    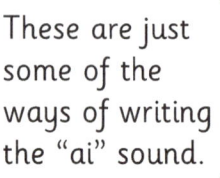

s**ai**lor   spr**ay**   w**a**v**e**   th**ey**

These are just some of the ways of writing the "ai" sound.

Now Try These

1. Say the words below. Circle the sound you can hear in all three words.

toy   point   voyage   "oi"   "ai"

2. Colour the beach balls that have words with the "ai" sound on them.

sway   tan   brave   loyal

3. Draw lines to match each word to the sound it contains.

play   spade   royal   joy

"oi"   "ai"

4. Underline the words in the sentence below that contain the "ai" sound. Then, write them on the dotted lines.

Kate was afraid of the grey shark in the sea that day.

....

....

An Extra Challenge

Ravi has written a diary entry about his day at the beach, but sand is covering some of the letters. Can you work out if each word is missing an "oi" sound or an "ai" sound?

Dear diary,

We are on holid⬚ at the seaside. The hotel we are st⬚ing in has ⬚t floors! Tod⬚ we went to the beach. It was very n⬚sy. I enj⬚ed lying in the sun, but the queue for the t⬚let was long.

Are you feeling fine and sandy?
Tick a box to show how you did.

Short "u" and short "oo" sounds

How It Works

Say the two words below. Both words have the short "u" sound.

Now say these words. Both words have the short "oo" sound.

h**u**ngry   c**o**ver   st**oo**d   f**u**ll

Some people use the **short "oo" sound** for **all** of the words above, so don't worry if you **can't hear a difference** between the two sounds.

Now Try These

1. Circle the two words that contain the same sound as the **oo** in **stood**.

cookie   fork   glass   pudding

2. Say the sentences below. Circle the word in each sentence that contains the same sound as the **u** in **hungry**.

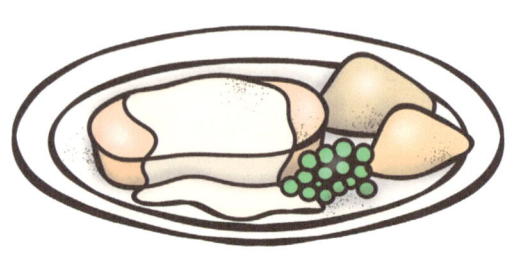

We all love eating pizza.

Clean under the table!

My uncle likes chicken.

3. Circle the words that contain the same sound as the **u** in **hungry**.

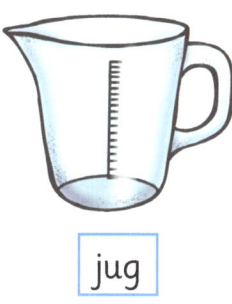   

jug   water   plum   menu

4. Fill the gap in each sentence with the word that contains the same sound as the **oo** in **stood**.

The waiter .... out the chair. | pulled | carried |

They buy meat from the .... | market | butcher |

They .... come here again. | would | will |

An Extra Challenge

Colin the cook is working in the kitchen. How many different things can you spot that use the short "u" or short "oo" sounds in the picture?

Were those pages to your taste?
Tick a box to show how you did.

29

Long "oo" and "yoo" sounds

How It Works

Have a go at saying these words. They all contain the long "oo" sound.

sc**oo**ter　　　gr**ou**p　　　s**ui**t　　　bl**ue**

Now say these words with the "yoo" sound. Each word has a different spelling.

 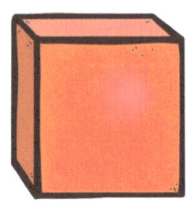 

arg**ue**　　　c**u**b**e**　　　n**ew**

Now Try These

1. Colour the blocks that have words with the long "oo" sound on them.

   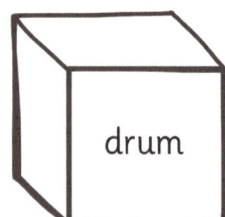

glue　　　puppet　　　broom　　　drum

2. Say the words below. Put a tick under the words that have the "yoo" sound.

  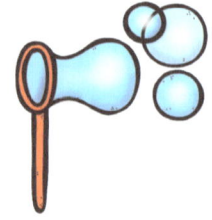 

stew　　　duck　　　bubble　　　cue

☐　　　☐　　　☐　　　☐

3. Circle the sound that's missing from all three words below.

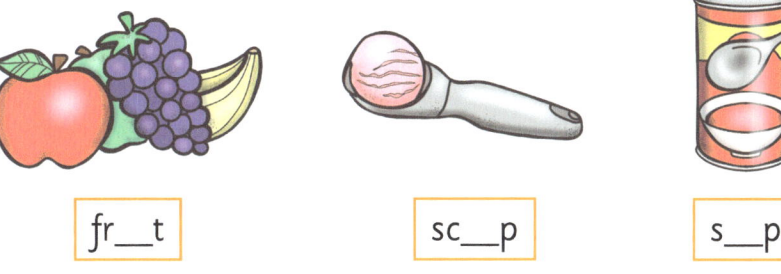

fr__t   sc__p   s__p

long "oo"

"yoo"

4. Practise reading the sentences below out loud. Circle the word in each sentence that contains the "yoo" sound.

Ernie counts a few marbles.

Rose has a huge teddy bear.

An Extra Challenge

Ella has lost her friend's birthday wish list. All she knows is that he asked for presents with the long "oo" sound in. What things can you spot in the toy shop that Ella could buy him?

Did you have fun playing with those sounds? Tick a box.

"ee" and "igh" sounds

How It Works

Practise saying the words below. They all have the "ee" sound.

gr**ee**n　　　s**ea**t　　　athl**ete**　　　mudd**y**

Now say these words. Each word has a different spelling of the "igh" sound.

h**igh**　　　m**i**c**e**　　　cr**y**

These are just some of the ways of writing each sound.

Now Try These

1. Say the words below. Put a tick under the words that contain the "ee" sound.

extreme　　　happy　　　kick

☐　　　☐　　　☐

2. Circle the word that contains the "igh" sound.

tree　　　grip　　　hide

3. Say the words below. Circle the sound that all of the words contain.

spider   bright   fly

"ee"

"igh"

4. Read the words below out loud.
   Colour in the pictures that have the "ee" sound.

leap   spin   three

An Extra Challenge

Amad is playing a game of "I spy" in the park. He's thinking of a word that contains the "igh" sound. Can you name all the words he could be thinking of from the picture below?

Did your eye spy all the right answers? Tick a box.

"sh", "zh" and "z" sounds

How It Works

Say the words with the "sh" sound. Each word spells the "sh" sound differently.

ship   **s**ugar   direc**ti**on   man**si**on   so**ci**al

Now say these words.
They both have a "zh" sound.

Practise reading these words.
They both have a "z" sound.

trea**s**ure   vi**si**on   li**z**ard   applau**se**

Now Try These

1. Read these words out loud. Colour the words that have the "sh" sound.

pincers   shell   lotion

2. Say the words below. Circle the word that has the "z" sound.

skull   cheese   sea

3. Fill the gap in each sentence with the word that contains the "sh" sound.

Percy is a pirate ……………………………… . nurse   chef

He cooks ……………………………… food. delicious   tasty

He always serves large ……………………………… . meals   portions

4. Circle the word in each sentence that has the "zh" sound in.

I heard an explosion !

There has been a collision .

An Extra Challenge

Captain Jim has used this map to find a treasure chest. To open the chest, he must think of five words that contain the "sh" or "zh" sound. Can you help?

How arrrgh you getting on with those sounds? Tick a box.

Answers

Pages 2-3 — i, o and e

1. wizard —  child —

2. monster —  ghost —

3. You should have coloured: <u>e</u>lf, w<u>e</u>ll
4. You should have circled: m<u>e</u>

   An Extra Challenge

   Same sound as the 'i' in 'w<u>i</u>ng': <u>i</u>nsect
   Same sound as the 'i' in 'f<u>i</u>nd': sp<u>i</u>der
   Same sound as the 'o' in 'fr<u>o</u>g': fr<u>o</u>g's, l<u>o</u>g
   Same sound as the 'o' in '<u>o</u>pen': potat<u>o</u>, tomat<u>o</u>
   Same sound as the 'e' in 'sp<u>e</u>ll': ins<u>e</u>ct, l<u>e</u>g

Pages 4-5 — u and a

1. You should have circled: p<u>a</u>per
2. You should have coloured: <u>u</u>niform
3. drum —
4. You should have circled: w<u>a</u>nts

   An Extra Challenge

   Same sound as the 'a' in 'pi<u>a</u>no':
   h<u>a</u>ppy, cl<u>a</u>p, t<u>a</u>p
   Same sound as the 'a' in 'r<u>a</u>dio': am<u>a</u>zing
   Same sound as the 'a' in 'w<u>a</u>tch': wh<u>a</u>t

Pages 6-7 — c, g and ch

1. garden —

   garage —

   gym —

2. You should have coloured: <u>c</u>abbage, <u>c</u>arrots
3. Jo had a tooth <u>a</u>che. — me<u>ch</u>anic
   Bart helps <u>ch</u>ildren. — tea<u>ch</u>er
   Sita uses ma<u>ch</u>ines. — <u>ch</u>ef

   An Extra Challenge

   Same sound as the 'g' in 'golf':
   <u>g</u>old, <u>g</u>reen, <u>g</u>rey
   Same sound as the 'g' in 'magic': oran<u>g</u>e

Pages 8-9 — ea, ow and ie

1. You should have circled: d<u>ea</u>d
2. Same sound as the 'ie' in 'p<u>ie</u>': repl<u>ie</u>d
   Same sound as the 'ie' in 'f<u>ie</u>ld': ch<u>ie</u>f, bel<u>ie</u>ve
3. Dex <u>mow</u>s the grass. — gr<u>ow</u>
   The tree fell <u>down</u>. — fl<u>ow</u>er
   They saw a <u>cow</u>. — fl<u>ow</u>er
4. b<u>ea</u>k — h<u>ea</u>t
   <u>ow</u>l — br<u>ow</u>n
   t<u>ie</u> — fl<u>ie</u>s

   An Extra Challenge

   Same sound as the 'ea' in 'l<u>ea</u>f':
   t<u>ea</u>pot, ice cr<u>ea</u>m
   Same sound as the 'ea' in 'w<u>ea</u>ther':
   f<u>ea</u>ther, br<u>ea</u>d

Pages 10-11 — y, er and ou

1. You should have circled: dr<u>y</u>
2. You should have coloured: h<u>ou</u>se, c<u>ou</u>nt
3. You should have ticked: sw<u>er</u>ve, f<u>er</u>n
4. My drill is l<u>ou</u>d.
   That is my spann<u>er</u>.
   The nails are rust<u>y</u>.

   An Extra Challenge

   Any sensible words from the picture that have the same sound as the 'er' in 'water', e.g. rul<u>er</u>, highlight<u>er</u>, sharpen<u>er</u>, pap<u>er</u>

Answers

Pages 12-13 — "f", "w" and "s" sounds

1. "f" — gra__ph__, __f__older
   "s" — pen__c__il, __s__tapler
2. You should have underlined:
   __s__trawberry, __s__andwich, jui__c__e
3. You should have written the words:
   __Wh__en, __wh__istle, __W__ill's, __w__on

   An Extra Challenge

   Any words with 'ph' in, e.g.
   ele__ph__ant, __ph__one, ne__ph__ew, __ph__oto, gra__ph__

Pages 14-15 — "e", "i" and "o" sounds

1. You should have circled: the "o" sound
2. You should have circled: dr__o__p
3. You should have coloured: h__ea__d, p__e__t
4. You should have underlined and written:
   T__i__m, m__y__stery, m__i__ssing, ch__i__ps

   An Extra Challenge

   There are six words: Fr__e__sh, r__ea__dy, b__e__st, T__e__n, h__ea__venly, br__ea__th

Pages 16-17 — "or", "ar" and "ur" sounds

1. You should have circled: "or"
2. You should have circled: f__a__ther, d__a__rk
3. You should have circled: h__ur__t, g__ir__l
4. c__a__lm — "ar"
   f__our__ — "or"
   h__ear__d — "ur"

   An Extra Challenge

   "ar" sound: c__a__r, p__a__rk, l__a__rge, f__a__rm, p__a__th (in some accents)
   "ur" sound: T__ur__n, f__ir__

Pages 18-19 — Space adventures

"yoo" — resc__ue__, h__u__man, f__u__mes f__u__ture
"igh" — sh__i__ne, m__i__nd, sk__ies__, fl__igh__t
"ee" — bel__ie__f, galax__y__, dr__ea__m, d__ee__p
"or" — __or__bit, l__au__nch, cl__aw__, astron__au__t

You should have ticked:
Zig meets a space explorer.
There is a moon in the sky.

You should have written:
bl__ue__, s__ui__t, m__oo__n

Pages 20-21 — "j" and "ch" sounds

1. You should have coloured: __g__iraffe
2. sna__tch__, ske__tch__, fri__dge__
3. Larry the lion is in a ca__ge__.
   Larry hid behind a he__dge__.
   Larry __j__umped on a log.

   dan__g__er — "j"
   __j__ungle — "j"
   na__t__ure — "ch"
   scra__tch__ — "ch"
   crea__t__ure — "ch"

   An Extra Challenge

   "j" sound: __j__am, we__dge__s
   "ch" sound: signa__t__ure, __ch__icken, __ch__ips, pa__tch__
   Other foods with the "j" sound:
   e.g. __j__elly, __g__ingerbread, fu__dge__
   Other foods with the "ch" sound:
   e.g. __ch__ocolate, __ch__estnut, __ch__eese, pea__ch__

Pages 22-23 — "ear" and "air" sounds

1. __ear__muffs — "ear"
   b__are__ — "air"
   reind__eer__ — "ear"
   w__ear__ — "air"
2. You should have coloured: __y__ear
3. You should have circled: ch__air__, sc__are__d

   An Extra Challenge

   The odd words out are '__f__ear' and 's__h__are'.

Pages 24-25 — "ow" and "oa" sounds

1. You should have coloured: t__oa__st, bel__ow__, h__o__me
2. You should have drawn a line to: tr__ou__sers
3. You should have circled:
   'ow' in 't__ow__el', 'ow' in 'sh__ow__er', 'ou' in 'm__ou__th'
4. You should have ticked:
   He put his c__oa__t on.
   She waved from the wind__ow__.

   An Extra Challenge

   "ow" sound — cl__ou__ds, m__ou__se, f__ou__ntain
   "oa" sound — scarecr__ow__, rainb__ow__

Answers

Pages 26-27 — "oi" and "ai" sounds

1. You should have circled: "oi"
2. You should have coloured: sw<u>ay</u>, br<u>a</u>v<u>e</u>
3. pl<u>ay</u> — "ai"
   sp<u>a</u>d<u>e</u> — "ai"
   r<u>oy</u>al — "oi"
   j<u>oy</u> — "oi"
4. You should have underlined and written:
   Kate, afraid, grey, day

   An Extra Challenge

   "oi" sound — n<u>oi</u>sy, enj<u>oy</u>ed, t<u>oi</u>let
   "ai" sound — holid<u>ay</u>, st<u>ay</u>ing, <u>eigh</u>t, Tod<u>ay</u>

Pages 28-29 — Short "u" and short "oo" sounds

1. You should have circled: c<u>oo</u>kie, p<u>u</u>dding
2. You should have circled: l<u>o</u>ve, <u>u</u>nder, <u>u</u>ncle
3. You should have circled: j<u>u</u>g, pl<u>u</u>m
4. The waiter p<u>u</u>lled the chair.
   They buy meat from the b<u>u</u>tcher.
   They w<u>ou</u>ld come here again.

   An Extra Challenge

   Any sensible words from the picture with the short "u" or short "oo" sound in, e.g. gl<u>o</u>ve, <u>o</u>ven, b<u>oo</u>k, s<u>u</u>gar, c<u>oo</u>k, w<u>oo</u>d

Pages 30-31 — Long "oo" and "yoo" sounds

1. You should have coloured: gl<u>ue</u>, br<u>oo</u>m
2. You should have ticked: st<u>ew</u>, c<u>ue</u>
3. You should have circled: long "oo"
4. You should have circled: f<u>ew</u>, h<u>u</u>g<u>e</u>

   An Extra Challenge

   Any sensible words from the picture with the long "oo" sound in, e.g. st<u>oo</u>l, b<u>oo</u>ts, ball<u>oo</u>ns, h<u>oo</u>p, fl<u>u</u>t<u>e</u>

Pages 32-33 — "ee" and "igh" sounds

1. You should have ticked: extr<u>e</u>m<u>e</u>, happ<u>y</u>
2. You should have circled: h<u>i</u>d<u>e</u>
3. You should have circled: "igh"
4. You should have coloured: l<u>ea</u>p, thr<u>ee</u>

   An Extra Challenge

   Any sensible words from the picture with the "igh" sound in, e.g. b<u>i</u>k<u>e</u>, sl<u>i</u>d<u>e</u>, butterfl<u>y</u>, k<u>i</u>t<u>e</u>

Pages 34-35 — "sh", "zh" and "z" sounds

1. You should have coloured: <u>sh</u>ell, lo<u>ti</u>on
2. You should have circled: chee<u>se</u>
3. Percy is a pirate <u>ch</u>ef.
   He cooks deli<u>c</u>ious food.
   He always serves large por<u>ti</u>ons.
4. You should have circled: explo<u>s</u>ion, colli<u>s</u>ion

   An Extra Challenge

   Any five sensible words with the "sh" or "zh" sounds in, e.g. <u>sh</u>op, i<u>ss</u>ue, po<u>ti</u>on, deci<u>s</u>ion, ca<u>s</u>ual